Coming to America

Why Italian Immigrants Came to America

Lewis K. Parker

The Rosen Publishing Group's
PowerKids Press™
New York

Published in 2003 by The Rosen Publishing Group, Inc.
29 East 21st Street, New York, NY 10010

First Edition

Book Design: Erica Clendening and Mindy Liu

Photo Credits: Cover, p. 21 (center) © AP/WideWorld Photos; p. 5 © Michael Maslan Historic Photographs/Corbis; pp. 6, 10–11, 13 (inset), 17 Library of Congress, Prints and Photographs Division; pp. 7, 12–13, 14–15 © Hulton/Archive/Getty Images; pp. 8–9 Erica Clendening; p. 9 (top) © Corbis; p.16 courtesy Brooklyn Historical Society; pp. 18–19 Walter Sanders/Timepix; p. 20 Mary Fratini; p. 21 (top) © Ralph Morse/Timepix; p. 21 (bottom) © Rex Hardy Jr./Timepix

Library of Congress Cataloging-in-Publication Data

Parker, Lewis K.
Why Italian immigrants came to America / Lewis K. Parker.
    p. cm. — (Coming to America)
Summary: Explores Italian immigration to the United States from the 1850s to the present, and looks at the contributions of Italian Americans to the culture of the United States.
Includes bibliographical references and index.
ISBN 0-8239-6460-4 (library binding)
1. Italian Americans—History—Juvenile literature. 2. Immigrants—United States—History—Juvenile literature. 3. United States—Emigration and immigration—History—Juvenile literature. 4. Italy—Emigration and immigration—History—Juvenile literature. [1. Italian Americans—History. 2. Immigrants—History. 3. Italy—Emigration and immigration. 4. United States—Emigration and immigration.] I. Title.
E184.I8 P29 2003
304.8'73045—dc21

                                                    2002000112

Contents

Hard Times in Italy

In the late 1800s and early 1900s, life in Italy was hard. Many people did not have jobs or enough food to eat. At times, there was so little rain that farmers could not grow crops.

Poor children in Italy often had to beg for food, just to get something to eat.

During this time, earthquakes killed thousands of people living in Italy. Volcanoes erupted and killed more people and buried cities under tons of ash.

To find a better way of life, people from Italy began to come to the United States.

Mt. Vesuvius has erupted many times, destroying nearby cities.

The Fact Box

In 1908, a powerful earthquake rocked Italy. It caused a huge tidal wave. The tidal wave killed 100,000 people in one city.

An earthquake in San Remo, Italy, caused the roof of this church to fall in.

7

Early Italian Immigrants

The first Italian immigrants came to America in the early 1830s. They came on sailing ships. Many of them became fruit sellers in cities on the East Coast. Some grew grapes on the West Coast. Other Italian immigrants became fishermen along the Gulf and the Pacific Coasts of America.

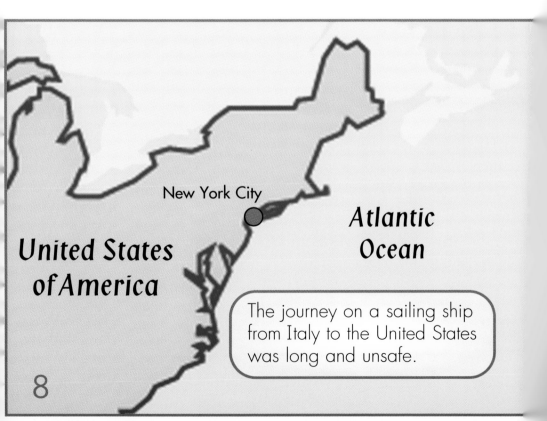

New York City

United States of America

Atlantic Ocean

The journey on a sailing ship from Italy to the United States was long and unsafe.

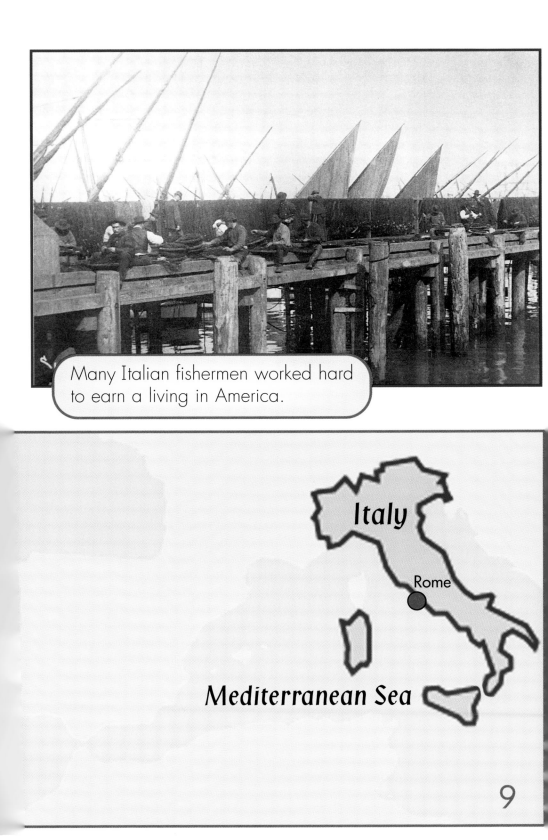

Many Italian fishermen worked hard to earn a living in America.

Italy

Rome

Mediterranean Sea

9

Traveling to America

Starting in the 1870s, most Italian immigrants traveled on steamships to get to America. They stayed below the ship's deck in small, crowded cabins.

Italian Immigration to the United States	
Year	Number
1851–60	9,000
1861–70	12,000
1871–80	56,000
1881–90	307,000
1891–1900	652,000
1901–10	2,046,000
1911–20	1,110,000
1921–30	455,000
1931–40	68,000
1941–50	57,000

Many people got sick on the trips.
Sailing to America took about
two weeks.

Immigrants were sometimes allowed to come
up on deck. There, they ate meals of soup and
stale bread. They could also enjoy fresh air.

Life in America

Most Italian immigrants were men between sixteen and forty-five years old. Many wanted to earn money in America and then return to their homes in Italy.

The first stop for many Italian immigrants was Ellis Island in New York City. Immigrants who were sick were not allowed into the United States and were sent back to Italy.

Other Italian immigrants wanted to save money to pay for their families to come to America. Italian immigrants often moved to large cities where they could find work as laborers.

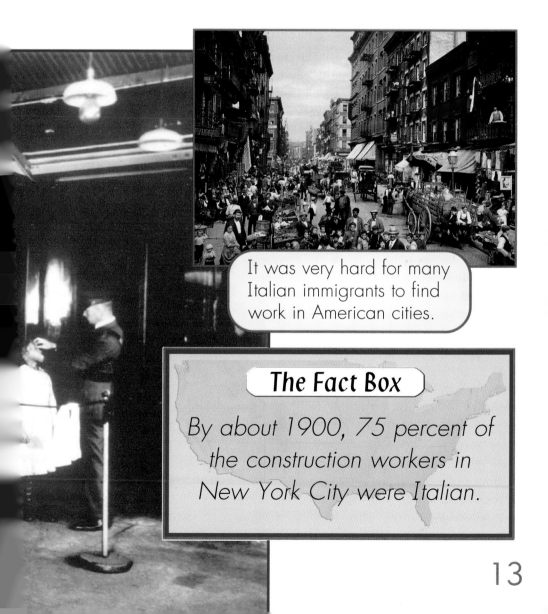

It was very hard for many Italian immigrants to find work in American cities.

The Fact Box

By about 1900, 75 percent of the construction workers in New York City were Italian.

13

Many Italian immigrants asked a padrone *(pah-DROH-nee)* to help them find work. A padrone was often another Italian immigrant who had come to America earlier. A padrone was paid money to find a job for an Italian immigrant.

Some Italian Americans sold fruits, vegetables, and fresh fish on the streets in many cities.

"I came to America because I heard the streets were paved with gold. When I got here, I found out three things: first, the streets weren't paved with gold; second, they weren't paved at all; and third, I was expected to pave them."

–Italian immigrant

Making and selling bread was another way some immigrants earned money.

Many Italian men worked in coal mines, factories, and rock quarries. They helped build railroads, tall buildings, bridges, tunnels, and subways.

These men helped to build the New York City subway.

Many Italian women sewed clothing at home to earn money. Children often sold newspapers. Many Italian Americans worked hard for low pay.

This woman is making money by sewing clothes at home.

By 1940, most Italian Americans lived in large cities, such as New York, Boston, and Chicago. Italian Americans had their own small communities in many of these cities.

Italian immigrants living in Boston's North End could buy the same food they had in Italy. Many Italian foods, such as pizza, spaghetti, ravioli, and lasagna, have become American favorites.

Italian Americans Today

Today, about 12 to 16 million Italian Americans live in the United States.

Italian Americans have become an important part of America.

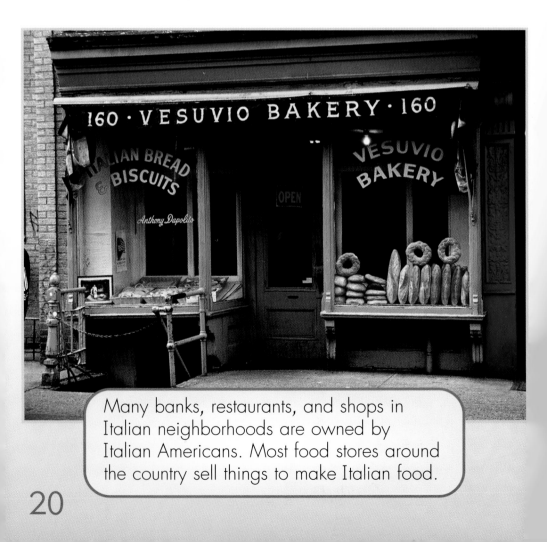

Many banks, restaurants, and shops in Italian neighborhoods are owned by Italian Americans. Most food stores around the country sell things to make Italian food.

In 1946, John Pastore of Rhode Island became the first Italian American to be a state governor. In 1950, he became the first Italian American senator.

Enrico Fermi was an Italian immigrant who came to the United States in the late 1930s. He is famous for his work with nuclear energy.

Frank Capra was an Italian immigrant who directed many famous American movies.

Glossary

ash (**ash**) what remains of something after it has been burned

earn (**uhrn**) to make money by working

earthquake (**uhrth**-kwayk) a shaking or moving of the ground

erupted (ih-**ruhp**-tihd) having thrown out with great force rock, hot ash, and lava from a volcano

immigrants (**ihm**-uh-gruhnts) people who come into a country to live there

laborers (**lay**-buhr-uhrz) people who do hard work with their hands

nuclear energy (**noo**-klee-uhr **ehn**-uhr-jee) a very strong source of power used to produce heat or make machines work

padrone (pah-**droh**-nee) a person who finds work for immigrants

quarries (**kwor**-ees) places where stone is dug, cut, or blasted out for use in making buildings

restaurants (**rehs**-tuh-rahnts) places to buy and eat a meal

tidal wave (**ty**-dehl **wayv**) a very high ocean wave, caused by an earthquake

volcano (vahl-**kay**-noh) an opening in the earth's crust through which rocks, steam, ash, and melted rock are sometimes forced out

Resources

Books

Italian Immigrants, 1880–1920
by Anne M. Todd
Capstone Press (2001)

The Italian American Family Album
by Dorothy Hoobler
Oxford University Press (1994)

Web Sites

Due to the changing nature of Internet links, PowerKids Press has developed an online list of Web sites related to the subjects of this book. This site is updated regularly. Please use this link to access the list:

http://www.powerkidslinks.com/cta/ita/

Index

Word Count: 388

Note to Librarians, Teachers, and Parents

If reading is a challenge, Reading Power is a solution! Reading Power is perfect for readers who want high-interest subject matter at an accessible reading level. These fact-filled, photo-illustrated books are designed for readers who want straightforward vocabulary, engaging topics, and a manageable reading experience. With clear picture/text correspondence, leveled Reading Power books put the reader in charge. Now readers have the power to get the information they want and the skills they need in a user-friendly format.